A Crabtree Branches Book

ANCIENT WARRIORS

BRAVE KNIGHTS

Thomas Kingsley Troupe

T0015068

Crabtree Publishing
crabtreebooks.com

School-to-Home Support for Caregivers and Teachers

This high-interest book is designed to motivate striving students with engaging topics while building fluency, vocabulary, and an interest in reading. Here are a few questions and activities to help the reader build upon his or her comprehension skills.

Before Reading:
- *What do I think this book is about?*
- *What do I know about this topic?*
- *What do I want to learn about this topic?*
- *Why am I reading this book?*

During Reading:
- *I wonder why...*
- *I'm curious to know...*
- *How is this like something I already know?*
- *What have I learned so far?*

After Reading:
- *What was the author trying to teach me?*
- *What are some details?*
- *How did the photographs and captions help me understand more?*
- *Read the book again and look for the vocabulary words.*
- *What questions do I still have?*

Extension Activities:
- *What was your favorite part of the book? Write a paragraph on it.*
- *Draw a picture of your favorite thing you learned from the book.*

TABLE OF CONTENTS

Into the Battle

The knight grips his lance, holding it close to his armored **torso**. He settles his horse and scans the battlefield. The enemy is advancing.

The commander gives his signal. The knight and the rest of the **order** ride into battle. As the mounted knights get closer, they lower their lances to attack!

What's a Knight?

Knights were mounted soldiers during the **Middle Ages**. Usually clad in armor, they were trained to serve their king or lord. Their job was to protect their land.

In late 11th century, knights became known for their **chivalry**. They followed rules to keep them from treating the less fortunate badly.

Fun Fact

Knights weren't always good guys. Before the late 11th century, they were known for being violent. They would steal and burn the villages where they fought in battles.

Knights began training as a page around age 7-10. A page was taught how to handle a horse, hunt, and fight with mock weapons. Pages served knights during this time.

From age 14, the page became a squire. A squire learned to use real weapons and started his education. Squires handled the knights' weapons and cleaned their armor.

Knight History & Life

Soldiers on horses have been around for thousands of years. The first true medieval knights appeared during the rule of King Charlemagne (768-814).

Known as Charles the Great, the knights kept him safe in battle. In return, the knights were given portions of the land they conquered. They were also paid with money and precious gifts.

Knights weren't always in battles to protect land or fight in **holy wars**. They very rarely saved damsels in distress.

To show their strength and valor, knights participated in contests. They could fight each other one on one or compete in a **joust** in front of crowds.

Knight Clothing

When a knight wasn't engaged in battle or in a tournament, they wore normal clothes. A **tunic**, trousers, and a pair of boots were all they needed.

For fighting, knights were clad almost head to toe in armor. Some knights wore plate armor made from metal pieces.

Fun Fact

Plate armor was made of separate pieces for the torso, arms, and legs. A full set of armor was heavy and could weigh between 45-55 pounds (20-25 kg)!

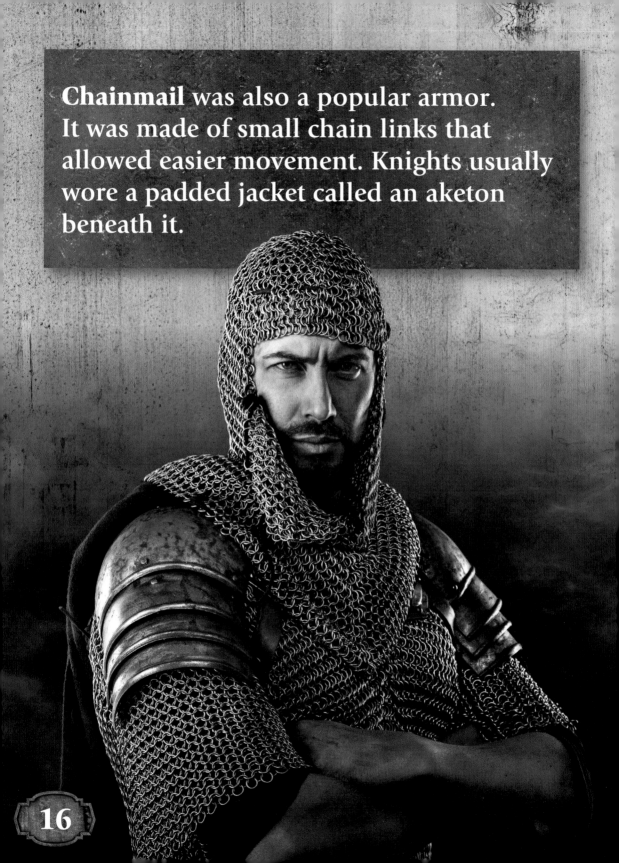

Chainmail was also a popular armor. It was made of small chain links that allowed easier movement. Knights usually wore a padded jacket called an aketon beneath it.

Knights also wore steel or iron helmets to protect their head and face. Some helmets had symbols or crests from their kingdom painted on them.

Knight Weapons

No knight would go into battle empty-handed. Most knights carried the sword given to him when he became a knight. Swords were long, heavy, and sharp and could do a lot of damage.

Because the enemy also carried swords, most knights also carried a shield with them. The knight's **heraldry** symbols were often painted on the front.

Fun Fact

Many knights wore a surcoat, or coat of arms, over their armor. The coat had a family symbol on it. Many knights also wore this symbol on their shield and horses. It helped other knights recognize them in battle.

A knight might also have a dagger, or a miniature version of their sword, on them. This was a weapon of last resort if their sword was dropped in battle.

Fun Fact

The arbalest, a type of crossbow, was used by knights in Europe starting in the 12th century. It could fire bolts accurately up to 110 yards (100 m).

Some knights used lances when riding on horseback into battle. Others, preferred a heavy club-like weapon called a mace. Some mace heads had spikes on them!

Knight Fighting

At the beginning of a battle, a knight would ride toward an enemy on his horse. Using his lance, he would try to spear his opponent.

The blow could kill the other or simply knock him off his horse. The lance wasn't much use after the first attack. The knight could attack from horseback and jump down to finish the fight.

When fighting with swords, knights tried to find weak points in their enemy's armor. They would swing and stab at enemies to do as much damage as possible.

During battle, if a knight lost his sword, he could use his shield as a weapon. A heavy shield blow could easily knock down an opponent.

Knights Today

With the invention of firearms, the knights in armor swinging swords slowly became history. By the end of the 15th century, countries relied mostly on their **infantry**.

However, people are still "knighted" today. Important men and women are sometimes given an honorary knighthood. The title of "Sir" is given to men and "Dame" is given to women.

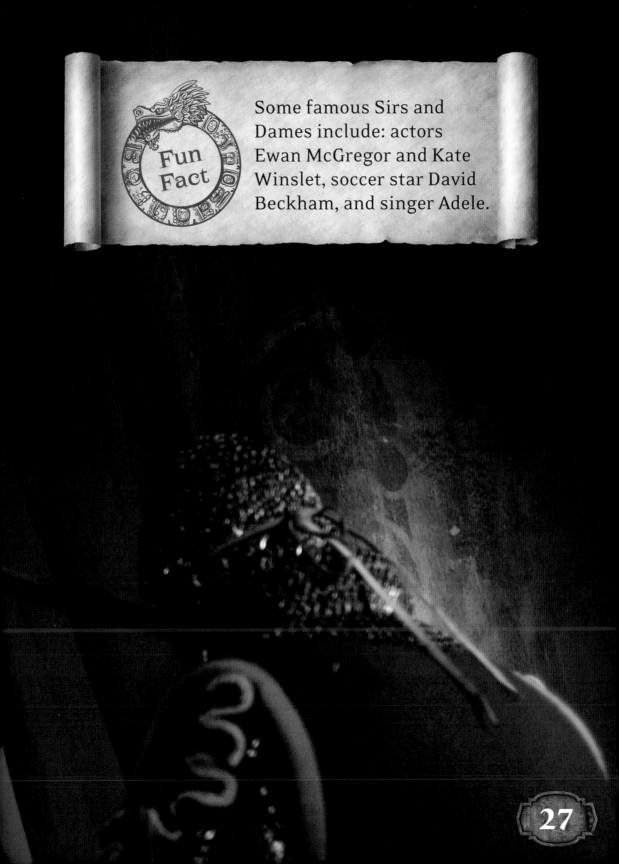

Fun Fact

Some famous Sirs and Dames include: actors Ewan McGregor and Kate Winslet, soccer star David Beckham, and singer Adele.

Even today, knights are remembered as brave fighters and heroes. Stories of their battles, swordsmanship, and chivalry have been passed down in literature through the ages.

Their place in history is still celebrated. Knights will always be remembered as the bravest and most loyal of ancient warriors!

Glossary

chainmail (CHAYN-mayl) Armor made of small metal rings linked together in a pattern to form a mesh of small chains

chivalry (SHI-vuhl-ree) A code of behavior for a knight during the Middle Ages in Europe, calling for courage, honor, manners, and charity

heraldry (HEH-ruhl-dree) A set of rules about the design and use of a knight's or noble's family coat of arms

holy wars (HOH-lee wawrz) Wars waged to support a religion

infantry (IN-fuhn-tree) Soldiers that fight on foot

joust (JOWST) Contest on horseback between two knights with lances

Middle Ages (MID-l eyjs) A period of history in Europe between 500 to 1500 C.E.

order (OR-dr) A group of persons with common interests

realm (RELM) A royal kingdom

torso (TAWR-so) The middle part of the human body

tunic (TU-nihk) A long shirt that hangs to the knees

Index

Websites to Visit

https://www.ducksters.com/history/middle_ages/knight_armor_and_weapons.php

https://www.ducksters.com/history/middle_ages/knight_coat_of_arms.php

https://www.youtube.com/watch?v=pG0dMxybV_8
[Video of life of a medieval knight]

About the Author

Thomas Kingsley Troupe is the author of over 200 books for young readers. When he's not writing, he enjoys reading, playing video games, and investigating haunted places with the Twin Cities Paranormal Society. Otherwise, he's probably taking a nap or something. Thomas lives in Woodbury, Minnesota, with his two sons.

Written by: Thomas Kingsley Troupe
Designed by: Bobbie Houser
Series Development: James Earley
Proofreader: Kathy Middleton
Educational Consultant: Marie Lemke M.Ed.

Photographs:
Shutterstock: Vuk Kostic: cover, p. 1; zef art: p. 4-5; Szymon Kaczmarczyk: p. 5; Anton Vierietin: p. 6-7; Elena Sherengovskaya: p. 8; Mihai Lucit: p. 9; St. Nick: p. 10-11; Vladimir Wrangel: p. 12-13; PRESSLAB: p. 14; Nomad_Soul: p. 15; alessandro guerriero: p. 16; knipsdesign: p. 17; Gorodenkoff: p. 18-19; Sibrikov Valery: p. 20; Warm_Tail: p. 21; St. Nick: p. 22-23; Gorodenkoff: p. 24-25, 28-29; Nejron Photo: p. 26-27

Crabtree Publishing

crabtreebooks.com   800-387-7650
Copyright © 2024 Crabtree Publishing

Printed in the U.S.A./072023/CG20230214

Published in Canada
Crabtree Publishing
616 Welland Ave.
St. Catharines, Ontario
L2M 5V6

Published in the United States
Crabtree Publishing
347 Fifth Ave
Suite 1402-145
New York, NY 10016

Library and Archives Canada Cataloguing in Publication
Available at Library and Archives Canada

Library of Congress Cataloging-in-Publication Data
Available at the Library of Congress

Hardcover: 978-1-0398-0946-8
Paperback: 978-1-0398-0999-4
Ebook (pdf): 978-1-0398-1105-8
Epub: 978-1-0398-1052-5